MW00463724

Acknowledgments

Thanks to Jan Hartman, who had the original vision for this book, to Kristen Hewitt at Princeton Architectural Press for her incisive editing, to the contributing writers who enabled me to see the natural world through their eyes, and to Ralph Waldo Emerson whose words continue to inspire us.

Published by
Princeton Architectural Press
202 Warren Street
Hudson, New York 12534
www.papress.com

ISBN 978-1-61689-986-8

Editor: Kristen Hewitt
Designer: Paula Baver

Library of Congress Control Number:
2020950585

Sign Language

Sign Language

by
Eliza Rhodes

To Carol & Shawn

Forward

One sunshiny day as I was approaching my favorite coffee shop I came upon the owner, Carol, positioning a sidewalk sign out front. The sign looked to be antique, and fit in quite well with the aesthetic of the Victorian building that houses the shop.

I said, "Cute sign, Carol," because it was actually cute somehow.

Standing back to admire it, Carol replied, "I know. I love it."

I asked, "What are you going to do with it?"

She said, "I don't know."

"Well, I'm sure it will come to you," I said as I walked up the steps to go inside.

A couple of days later, as I took the first sip of my daily Chai tea, Carol approached me rather intently.

She said, "Shawn has an idea about what to do with the sign." Shawn is Carol's husband, and they own the shop together. "He said that you will write something on the sign every day, and we will pay you for it in Chai tea."

"I'll do it," I agreed immediately, because I instantly loved the idea of being paid to do anything in Chai tea— so ridiculous and wonderful. Then the very next thing out of my mouth was, "Wait, you want me to do what? Write what?"

Carol's response, which is so Carol, by the way, was, "Oh, you know. Just whatever you'd write."

"Uhhh, alright," I said.

I had no idea where that brief conversation would lead. I figured I would think of something to write on the sign the first few days, and then defer to Mark Twain and Oscar Wilde. Well, I found that I had more than a few days worth of things to say. In fact, it turns out that I am quite chatty. This book is filled with things that I have written on the sign.

I think it is very important to note, and surely this first thing goes without saying, that I am not the Dalai Lama. I do not have a television show. I am not a psychiatrist, a psychologist, or a degree holder in ancient Greek philosophy. I cannot touch the tip of my nose with my tongue. I have worked mostly as a waitress, and I am a good hula hooper, for whatever that's worth.

The reason I mention all of this is that I believe inner peace is a lot more widely available than most of us may think. It is something that I have been looking for, and dontcha know that where I've been finding it is right here inside of me. Some days I do not find it as quickly or easily as I do other days. I have learned something very valuable from those more challenging times. When I am struggling with thoughts or feelings that are less than peaceful I ask myself, "What *should* I be thinking? What is the lesson here that I *could* be learning?" I turn the thought upside down. And poof! It is like magic how well that works for me.

Perhaps I catch myself feeling grouchy. I ask myself what that's about. I may find the root of it is that I am feeling impatient. Then I know that my lesson is patience. And somehow even just getting that far helps. Then I ponder on patience, and that is what I will go write about on the sign. Certainly it is not necessary to write on a sidewalk sign in front of a coffee shop in order to derail an unproductive thought– that just happens to be how I came by the process.

This job that I get paid for in tea has been such an unusual and wondrous opportunity. It has forced (read allowed) me on a daily basis to look at things differently– more closely. As improbable as it is, through a sign on a sidewalk I am gaining a better understanding of the world, of people, of myself.

I hope you too will find something inside this book, but more importantly, inside yourself, that will bring you further peace and joy.

–Eliza Rhodes

If you can't
laugh it off
try laughing harder.

Do we really need
to traverse
all of Oz
killing witches & whatnot
to learn that
we've had the power
all along?

It is
what it is,
and it isn't
what it isn't.

There's a lot
to admire
in the straightforward
communication
of a wagging tail.

HELP PUT A STOP
TO WRONGDOING
by doing
the right thing.

Your mind may
lead you astray,
but your heart
will show you
the way.

Integrity:
Happening even
when no one
is looking.

LOST: Temper—
short, nasty,
irrational
IF FOUND: Please
do not take
personally

The most surefire
way to bring love
into your life
is to be loving.

Many of my days
have taken a turn
for the better
with the help
of just one smile.
Usually, my own.

When assessing
one's abilities
don't confuse
can't with haven't.

Do not underestimate

the power of

words not spoken.

Friendship is like
a lot of things
in a way.
If you treat
it well—
it lasts longer.

When you're grumpy,
and you don't feel
like being nice, but
you're nice anyway—
you get extra credit.

There may be
many different paths
leading to success—
giving up
does not appear
to be one of them.

At the very least,
looking on
the bright side
offers a
better view.

If you have
a good sense
of humor
things don't even
need to be
going so well.

We're all
in it
together.
Act
accordingly.

Kindness
doesn't need
a reason.

You can tell a lot
about a person
by whether
they prefer
Tug-O-War or
Twister.

Be the light
at the end
of the tunnel.

You can talk
someone's ear off,
but I don't think
that you could
listen someone's
mouth off

The right way
isn't always
the most popular.

When you speak
the truth
you may be
surprised to see
who stops to listen.

Somehow you
end up
getting more
when you give
more than
you take.

New Diet:
Think more about
what comes out
of your mouth
than you do about
what goes in it.

As kids it was
acceptable practice
to call for
a "do over."
...maybe, we
should reinstate
that practice.

Don't even give
Can't
the time of day.

Thinking positive
thoughts about
the future
pays off right now—
regardless of what
actually happens then.

We don't get
stuck in traffic
when we take
the high road.

A change in perspective
can happen anywhere.
It's not necessary
to travel to
exotic locales, though,
the postcards
would be better.

Beautiful, wondrous,
and magical things
happen every day
whether you notice
them or not.

Attendance
counts
toward
your
grade.

Most of us make BOTH
of the following mistakes:
1) Think that we're
more important than we
are.
2) Think the opposite.

Unlike Algebra,

once you

learn patience

you still continue

to be tested for it.

FASHION TIP:
Everyone
looks better when
they're wearing
a smile.

Perseverance
is always
rewarded.

Being pleasant

is a

public service.

Encourage,
extol, and
express
enthusiasm!

Gentleness
can be
very powerful.

Think how much
beauty would be
missed if
the autumn leaves
resisted change
the way we
so often do.

When confronted
with adversity
my Grandma
would always advise
in her gentle
Southern accent,
"You've just got to
riiise above it."

Many very
possible things
were once
thought impossible.

To unclutter a mind
(or a closet)
get rid of
things that
no longer suit you,
or never really worked
in the first place.

If you are your
own worst enemy—
once you overcome
yourself
you will be met
with surprisingly
few obstacles.

Do you
want to catch
what you're chasing?

Thankfully,
Neil Armstrong
didn't fall for
that old line,
"The sky's the limit."

The Final Frontier

may be

interior.

Don't spend the day
thinking about
how dark it was
last night.

You are what
you ~~eat~~ think.
Avoid thinking
junk thoughts
that fill you up,
but aren't
good for you.

It is not necessary
to move a mountain
to get to
the other side of it.

What makes
possibilities
possible
are people
like
us.

Endurance:
Some problems
can be overcome
merely by
outlasting them.

Let your doubts
sit back & watch
while you
take their dare.

You don't have to
be rich, famous,
tall, thin, young,
or good looking
to be kind—
anyone can do it.

Open your heart—
there may be
someone waiting
to get in

Tell
yourself
the
truth.

One of the
nicest things
anyone ever
said to me
was a hug.

The more open
the mind—
the bigger
the ideas
it can
accommodate.

If you can look
inside yourself to
call up courage once—
from then on
you'll have
the number handy.

Even a rear view mirror
will tell you that
things are not
always as
they appear.

Exceed

your

potential.

More people have
achieved success
due to their
tenacity than
their luck.

Love always
leaves clues.
It wants to
be found.

Words can be
a form of litter
to which the
old idea applies—
leave a place
better than
you found it.

Surprise
yourself.

A thoughtful little
gesture is rarely
seen as small
by the one
being thought of

Food soaks up
and takes on
the qualities of
the marinade.
We do too.
Be mindful of
your marinade.

Fear is a
backseat driver
who speaks up
far more often
than is necessary.

Do you *literally* drive in the opposite direction you need to go, because that way is easier to travel? Do you do it *figuratively*?

We can find
something beautiful
everywhere we
look for it.

Hurt or frightened
animals sometimes
lash out even at
those trying to
care for them.
Realizing— aren't we
all like this?
Compassion &
forgiveness arise.

The more we
can find joy
in common things
the more commonly
we'll be joyful.

Apology is
more honorable
than denial.

We can look
for happiness
in where we go,
but we can
find it in
how we go.

Apathy is
the name of
the slow boat
to nowhere.

Just because you're
not facing reality
doesn't mean
that reality
isn't facing you.

Trees do not become
too scared to
branch out & grow.
Trees are
good teachers.

Put a stop
to
what's stopping
you.

If you keep at it
till you
learn something
there will be
success in
everything you do.

Making an attempt
does not guarantee
you'll attain it,
however, there is
a guarantee if you
do not attempt.

When we speak
to someone
from our heart—
they will often
listen to us
from theirs.

If there's enough time
to do what you
should have done—
do it.
If there's
not enough time—
do it faster.

Are you behaving
like someone
who has
their priorities
in proper order?

Our circumstances
are mostly
more fluid
than we realize,
and our reactions are
mostly more concrete
than is beneficial.

The right thing
isn't always the
easiest to enact,
but it is
always the easiest
to live with

The most essential
element of flying
is the courage to
leave the ground.

Wisdom

is

aging's reward.

Make opportunity
want to
come knocking.

If you want to
catch a plane—
don't wait for it
at the bus station.

The best
time machine
would truly
bring us all
to the present.

We can't
change the truth
by not telling it.

The person who
invented recess
was no less brilliant
than the ones who
invented long division
and lunchtime.

Sometimes
we open a door,
sometimes
a door opens us.

Weeds or wildflowers?
It all depends
on how you
look at it.

It's sensible to
anchor your boat
in calm waters
instead of rough.
It's the same
with your mind.

Listen then decide,
because most of us
don't listen
after we've decided.

When we look

at the face

of the person

blocking our way

we see that

it is our own.

Tides always turn.
When they come in
we can
enjoy the swim.
When they go out
we can
bask in the sun.

When properly
substituted with
the word "growth,"
change is
not so scary.

Unless you
let go of
the ball you caught
in the first inning—
your hands won't be free
to catch any
in the rest of the game.

Friendliness
actually seems to
reap more
than it sows.

The more you
fill your head with
creative imaginings
the less room
there'll be for
needless worrying.

Do caterpillars
drag their little
caterpillar feet,
because they
don't want to
become butterflies?
Should we?

Live the present
so that in the future
when you
talk about the past
it makes a good story.

Life is an ocean
of opportunities.
You can choose
to let the waves
pass you by, or
you can ride them.

My refrigerator,
my car, & you
all have
an interior light
that shines
when open.

You think
you can.
Another thinks
you can't.
Only one of you
is right,
and it's probably
you.

Be
what
you're
looking
for

Of the following
magic words
one remains
exceedingly effective:
*Abracadabra
*Allakhazam
*Presto
*Open Sesame
*Please

There's lots of talk about having to learn to say, "no," but it seems that most of us need to learn to say, "yes."

A tall palm tree
surrenders to
the changes
in the wind,
and by bending
does not fall.

Have the strength
to stand your ground,
and the courage
to change your mind.

The Truth
always has
your best interest
at heart.

The difference
between being
in a rut, and
being in the groove
is attitude.

Will

the real you

please stand up

Peace, love, &
volcanic eruptions
are all big things
that happen from
the inside out

As with climate—
a sunny & warm
disposition is
easier to enjoy.

It is usually
simpler
than we make it.

A true friend
will stand with you
against your enemies—
most especially when
your enemy is you.

It is more
gratifying to
build a bridge
than a wall.

Doing the right thing
keeps you on
the right track
which puts you in
the right place
at the right time.

Advice from a flower:
One is not meant
to stay a rosebud—
one is meant to
open up & bloom.

A change in
perspective can have
an extraordinary effect—
just look at Picasso.

Drama
makes a
better movie
than a
lifestyle.

If you can't
find a way,
find a way
around it.

Optimizing
is more
fun than
pessimizing.

Despite what
Orthodontists may say—
with smiling quantity
is, ultimately,
more important
than quality.

Are we really
doing something
with our lives,

or are we

just trying
to look busy?

Fresh starts
are available
every moment.

Both success & failure
are teachers
who will teach
absolutely anyone
who is willing
to learn.

When the bar
has been raised
resist the temptation
to limbo under it.

On encouragement:
It can warm
your heart
to fan the flames
of another's fire.

Physical strength
is increased by
working at it—
as is inner strength.

The top of
Mt. Everest isn't
reached at a sprint,
rather with many
small slow steps.

We must all carry
our own load, but
a friend can
talk us out
of over packing.

Open hearts open minds.

We can

fear the unknown,

or we can

look forward

to making

its acquaintance.

When we
better ourselves
we better
our world.

We find unexpected
plot twists in movies
interesting & exciting—
we can choose
to view life
like that too.

Unless you
are smiling
there's a chance
you're taking it
too seriously.

You always have
the option to
choose what would
be best for you.

Go in
hot pursuit
of your dreams.

Forgiveness
frees
the forgiven &
the forgiving.

Wisdom from a
Help Wanted sign:
Inquire Within

Just deciding to
face your fear
starts to make
it disappear.

Sometimes it requires

a leap of faith

just to take

a step

in the right direction.

Where are you dwelling?
The Neighborhood of
Possibilty, or the
Valley of Discontent?

location location
location

We all get to
pick our part—
Ray of Sunshine
or
Dark Cloud.

If something
needs doing
do it.

When faced with
the choice between
this & that—
don't disregard
the other thing.

What goes on
inside your head
determines where
you're headed.

Beware of:

*Taking on too much &
being overwhelmed

*Taking on too little &
being underwhelmed

We can choose to

raise our voices

to sing or to scold,

use our hands

to slap or to hold,

to have a

warm heart or cold.

When approached
with something new
do you bark or wag?

An explosive
personality can
express itself
as a pipe bomb
or fireworks.

Of all the
far off places
in the world—
one of the greatest
destinations is
the here & now.

If you try
something new &
fall on your face—
technically that is
still "moving forward."

Patience expands
the time table,
thus allowing
everything to
fall into place.

When you're
in turbulence
fly higher
up above it.

The sooner
we do
the right thing,
the sooner
things are right.

It is the
pearl inside,
not the shell,
that's impressive.

Feeding things
makes them grow.
Nourish the heart
not the ego.

Evolving

beats

the

alternative.

A good laugh
is like
a vacation.

It is within
that we find the
stormiest of seas, and
the safest of harbors.

You can't fail
if you
don't quit.

Wisdom from
the Hokey Pokey:
Put your
whole self in

The ability to
know when to
speak one's mind,
and when to
hold one's tongue
directly correlates to
one's popularity.

Secrets of Success from
The Little Engine
That Could:

1. Believe in yourself.

2. Stay on track.

We can always
work with what
we have, but
not with what
we wish we had.

Wish upon
yourself &
make your
dreams come true.

Be a pirate
of pleasantness—
spew niceties &
leave gladdened hearts
in your wake.

The same road
leads to
the same place.

Much like potatoes,

we better savor

success

when it's not

instant.

The sun
is always
shining
whether we
can see it
or not.

Train your thoughts
to stay
on the
sunny side
of the street.

If you
don't like
your choices
create
an alternative.

If we learn from
a bad experience—
it's not
a bad experience.

The sea is
not always as
rough as we
make it out to be—
mostly we rock
our own boat.

No amount

of beauty

is too small

to be enjoyed.

We can treat
our lives like
a good Mystery—
keep reading &
allow the story
to unfold without
getting stuck on just
one page's events.

When we look
for the good
in people
we find it.

There only is
what is.
There is no more
was.
What might be
is a figment
of your imagination.

It's not necessary
to tether
one's dreams—
they're meant
to take flight.

Art is
the result of
a heart
that has spoken.

Rarely is
the voice of reason
heard shouting.

It takes
the most courage
to stand up
to yourself.

Good humor,
like flying first class,
doesn't make
the trip shorter—
just more enjoyable.

Wisdom from a river:
No matter how many
twists & turns
you still
end up
in the right place.

When it's time
to sit down &
make a decision—
send your ego
out for sandwiches.

It's basic economics—
the more we
appreciate
the more valuable
we become.

Stretching ourselves
makes it easier
to reach
our goals.

We can
chart the course
only for so long—
then it is time
to set sail.

Just because
they wouldn't
doesn't mean
you couldn't.

Like a house guest—
the more
you entertain
a thought
the longer it stays,
and the more comfortable
it gets.

Wisdom from sports:
Even when
it looks like
you're losing
you can
still win.

The power of
a deep breath
really is
underrated.

Worrying is
an ineffective &
unpleasant attempt
at time travel.

Like it or not—

we are

far better served

by a

worthy opponent

than a

"yes man."

Very few things
are any real match
for
determination.

We can check on

ourselves by asking:

Will I want

to lie in

the bed

that I'm making?

Live today's
dreams today,
as there will be
new dreams
for tomorrow.

Our heart

tells us

the answer,

but sometimes

we don't hear it

over the

blah blah blah

coming from our head.

If you've yet
to master
the hocus pocus—
you can still
howl at the moon.

Kindness, humor,
and patience
will get you through
pretty much anything.

If we
put off
the attempt
we put off
the success.

When we stop
dragging our feet
we get a
spring in our step.

If you thought
you could get
whatever you
set your sights on
would you be
aiming higher?

Wisdom from a
three-legged race:
By working *with*
one another
we go farther faster.

Pay attention, because
keeping your eye
on the ball
sure beats
getting hit
in the head
with it.

All around us

poems are

writing themselves—

and they'll share them

with whomever

is listening.

When you are
the type of person
people can
count on—
you always have
someone you
can count on too.

Be mindful
of which fire
you're fueling.

Do what it
takes to get
clarity, and
then clarity
will take it
from there.

Every single story
of triumph
includes obstacles
that were overcome.

There's
a lot of
believe
in
achieve.

Optimism is
so fast acting
that it offers
immediate
benefit.

The bait
correlates
to the catch.
If you don't want
to catch
a worm eater
don't bait
your hook
with worms.

The sooner we
learn the lesson
the sooner we
graduate from
the problem.

That which is
truly important
makes for a
short list.

What might be,
might not be.

It may be helpful
to first ask,
"What is my motive
for doing this,
or saying that?"

The little
voice inside
doesn't have
the most lines
just
the best ones.

Life
is
a
surprise
party.

Uncertainty does
still leave
room for
a favorable
outcome.

Surpass
the
past.

Courtesy
to one's
fellow travelers
makes
the journey
easier on everyone.

Much can
be done
with a
level head,
and a
light heart.

We don't have to
wait for the wind
to change,
we can pick up
the oars & row.

Advice from the sun:
Be warm &
shine light on
everyone you
come across

If you
don't see
a silver lining
sew one in

Happiness is
always ripe
for the picking.

If ever
you lose
your way—
follow your heart.

There's nothing wrong
with being
trigger happy
when you're
shooting for the stars.

Ironically,
being selfless
actually
serves us
better than
being selfish.

Accept
merriment's
invitation.

A lazy day
is productive
in its own way.

Nobody's soul
has ever gotten
too fat—
keep yours
well fed.

Perhaps, like Columbus,

we need to

go out & look

for what we

suspect is there

beyond the horizon.

If we savor it
while it lasts,
it will last
long enough.

Believing in
possibility
dramatically increases
probability.

Those of us
employing a guard
at our heart
could see improvement
by reassigning them
to our mouth.

Swap out
childish
for childlike.

Integrity invites
a better class
of admirers.

Our best us

brings out

their best them.

Scars are
proof that
we can heal.

In all the years
my dog & I
have known each other
one of us
has never been grouchy.

The best thing
you can do
for your heart
is to use it.

Better to

jump for joy

than

to conclusions.

Relax into
yourself.

When you let go,
you are free.

Is what's
most important
to you
getting most of
your attention?

We can use the
ticking of time
for a beat
by which
to dance.

Wisdom from
a lighthouse:
Just standing tall
and shining your light
will help others to
find their way.

Take steps
that are
worth following.

Anger is fear
trying to hide
behind a
scary mask.

Some choose a
tranquil place
to vacation, others
a tranquil place
to live, others still
a tranquil state of mind.

Fortunate are we
to be helped
by another—
blessed are we
to be doing
the helping.

Every perfect solution
started out
as a problem.

Even a
small kindness
can make a
big impression.

Transcend

the

trivial.

Every thing that
doesn't work out
leads us closer
to what does.

Let your
imagination
turn to
innovation.

Lighten your heart,
lighten your load.

There is a
big difference
between
treading water &
drowned.

Common ground
allows
steadier footing
for everyone.

What we are
capable of achieving
is revealed through
our perseverance.

If you want
more flowers—
plant more seeds.

When you are
accustomed to
too much—
at first plenty
will seem like
not enough.

Ultimately, having
kept at it
will be easier
on us than
having given up

Simply by
being nice
you make
the world
a better place.

Be true,

and the rest

falls into place.

So powerful are
the effects of
good humor that
it need not even
be our own
to be enjoyed.

If we spend
our energy on
how we can,
instead of,
if we can—
we will.

Treating love
as an action
rather than
a concept
makes all
the difference.

Taking delight
in something
doesn't leave
any less of it.

Things are
nearly always
better than
they seem.

If taking on the
worries of the world
relieved the world
of its worries
there'd be nothing
left to worry.

Hindsight often reveals
that when
we didn't get
what we wanted—
we did.

If you
don't like

the way
things are going—
go another way.

It is in
the silence
that we
hear the most.

More good
comes from
lending your ear
than your money.

When you lead
your thoughts
you are not
at the mercy
of following them
wherever they go.

Everyone makes
a difference.
Are you making
the kind you'd
like to be?

Who

don't

you

think

you

are?

Be where
you are &
you'll have
gotten where
you're going.

Is it

as serious

as you're

making it?

You can't
get fat
by swallowing
your pride.

Rays of light
warm whomever
turns their face
up to meet them.

Wanna know
the answers?
Do your
homework.

Act with
kindness,
react with
kindness.

Honesty
is
bravery's
voice.

Life imitates art:

If you can't

make sense of

one or the other—

step back &

look again.

Oddly, it takes

less out of you

to do it

than to

put it off

Appreciate.

Much better

to be given

a slim chance

than

a fat chance.

Honor

the present

with

your presence.

When you believe
that every day
is a gift
life is
quite the party.

Chances are
whatever you're
looking for
is close at hand.

Be the

best case scenario.

Laughing
burns
calories.

Don't let
the fear of
what if
steal your
what is.

Inner beauty

attracts

the most beautiful people.

Lurking among
the unknown &
unexpected are
pleasant surprises.

When we feel
compassion
we act with
grace.

Insight from
a clothing tag:
Slight imperfections
and variances
contribute to
charm & uniqueness.

We don't have to
wait for
an occasion
to rise.

Get the most
out of today by
letting it be today.
Yesterday had
its chance.
Tomorrow can wait
its turn.

Anticipation can
be a bit of
a drama queen—
you'll get
the real story
from experience.

We can
liberate ourselves,
because we are
the ones
holding us
captive.

Some dreams
come true &
you do
have a say in
which ones.

Love who
you are,
love who
you aren't.

Beat yourself at
your own game.

The world record
distance for
spitting a
watermelon seed is
68 feet 9 1/8 inches
Set in 1989
by Lee Wheelis.

Would you
preach
what you're
practicing?

Good humor
makes
good company.

Those

in the know

live

in the now.

Often a
quiet truth
accompanies a
noisy diversion.

Thinking that
there's gotta be
a better way
is the beginning
of finding one.

Money makes for
a better vehicle
than it does
a driver.

What's worse than
being late for
your own funeral?
Being early.

Give each
new day
the chance to
fulfill its promise.

Improvement is
less commonly needed
in our aim
than in our
choice of target.

Once you know
where to go
all that's left
is the going.

Ever notice

how similar

the words

levity &

levitation are?

We get the
most out of it
by making
the most of it.

You already have
everything you need.

By making a habit
of doing our best
even our best
gets better.

The best possible outcome
of a decision
based on money
is money.
The best (*and* the worst)
possible outcome
of a decision
based on love
is love.

This phrase can
be added after
anything you do,
"and I lived happily
ever after."

Are you
thinking your thoughts,
or are you
letting your thoughts
think you?

We can

hem & haw

at the inconvenient,

balk at

the difficult,

or do

the impossible.

By letting go of
what weighs us down
we can't help but
to rise.

If you can't
right a left,
right a wrong.

Running to yourself
is more rewarding
than its opposite.

If you're
too busy
trying to steer
your tomorrow
whose driving
your today?

The difference
between
good enough &
giving it our all
is a choice.

If you can
make someone laugh—
you should.

There is
a freedom
in focus.

Serenity

is

underrated.

Keeping it simple
makes it easier
to find things
in your house,
your heart, and
your head.

If we always knew
what would
happen next—
the exhilaration
of being alive
would be
sadly sapped.

All winners
of races
have this
in common—
they dared to
cross the
starting line.

What would
be the point
of being
anything other
than optimistic?

Fresh air
will come in
through an
open window.

The more interest

we show in

the right thing

the more

the right thing

shows an interest

in us.

As long as
we're alive
we may as well
act like it.

Impatience:
The speeding up
of the process
by which
one becomes
unnecessarily
aggravated.

Taking a chance
can bypass
the need to
wait for
opportunity to
come knocking.

There is no law
that states that
you can't keep your
wits about you *and*
wear your heart
on your sleeve.

Time
added to
uncertainty
brings
understanding.

It is

more common to

be in a hurry

than it is

to know

where you're going.

Frustration

gives us

an edge

with which

to sharpen

our determination.

We win
the most
when we
go all in.

When we

are true

to our heart

we are free.

Do as much
as you can, and
be pleasantly surprised
by how much
you could.

We could view life
like a hike
where we enjoy all
that being out
on the trail entails—
uphill climbs,
rocky patches, and all.

It may be easier
to stand around
in the shallow end,
but learning to swim
in the deep end
is more exciting.

Recognize

your

blessings.

We can always
find trouble
when we look for it,
and the same goes
for its opposite.

Like the old game—
we can judge
how close we are
to what we're
looking for
by whether we feel
hot or cold.

Raise your sails
in preparation
for your windfall.

Caterpillar wisdom:

Once you

free yourself

from your

own cocoon

you can fly.

The mascot for
the Optimists Club
must be a
Can Can dancer.

Extra Special Thanks

To Carol, my fairy godmother, who continually uses her magic to better my life. Thank you for believing in me. Thank you for not ever seeming to use the word "can't." Thank you for EVERYTHING.

To Jessica Freeman who operates at such a high level of competency that only dogs & dolphins can hear it. I wouldn't be surprised to learn that she is responsible for the sun rising & setting on time every day.

To Joe Freeman whose willingness to help and unending patience have him on the fast-track to sainthood.

To the infamous David Cothran who, when he saw the old sign needed replacing, sneaked off & built a "new" one out of salvaged wood— some of which had been part of a house built over 100 years ago. I love that The Sign has its own history.

To the incredibly kind and very capable

Pieter who has been so helpful, and then even said that it was not necessary to thank him. Well, I couldn't quite help myself. THANK YOU!

To all the fabulistas & fabulistos who have worked behind the counter, and cheerfully been a daily part of it all.

To Alexis Miller for valiancy in the 11th hour.

To my father for always knowing that I could do it, and to my mother for being glad that I did.

And to all the readers of The Sign.